NATIONAL ANTHEM of SOUTH AFRICA

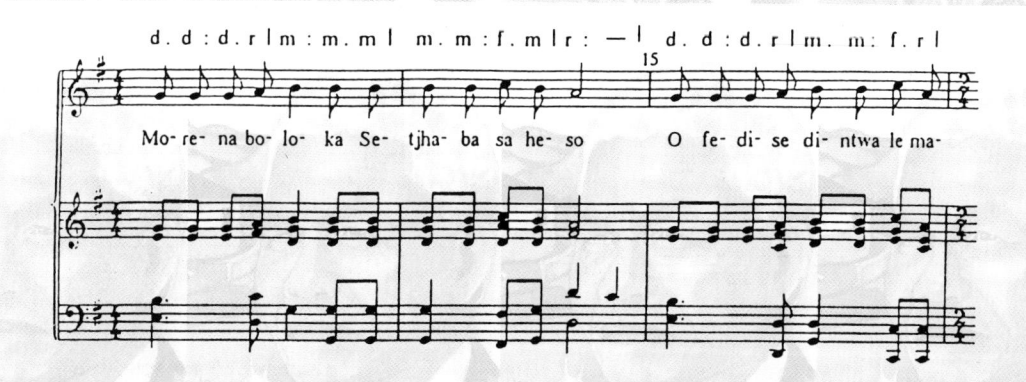

tshwe- nye- ho, O se bo- lo- ke   O   se bo- lo-

ke, Se- tjha- ba sa he- so,   Se- tjha- ba sa,   South A- fri-

Key of D

ka,   South A- fri- ka,   Uit die blou van on- se

he mel, uit die diep- te- van ons see,   oor ons

continued on back page

Published by Actua Press ©

Copyright 1998

All rights reserved

First Impression 1998
Second Impression 2000
Third Impression 2000
Fourth Impression 2002
Fifth Impression 2006
ISBN 1-86815-313-4

Printed and bound by
Interpak Books, Pietermaritzburg

MADIBA – THE STORY OF NELSON MANDELA

by

Chris du Toit

Illustrations

Friedel Eloff

ACTUA PRESS

CHILDREN'S BOOKS

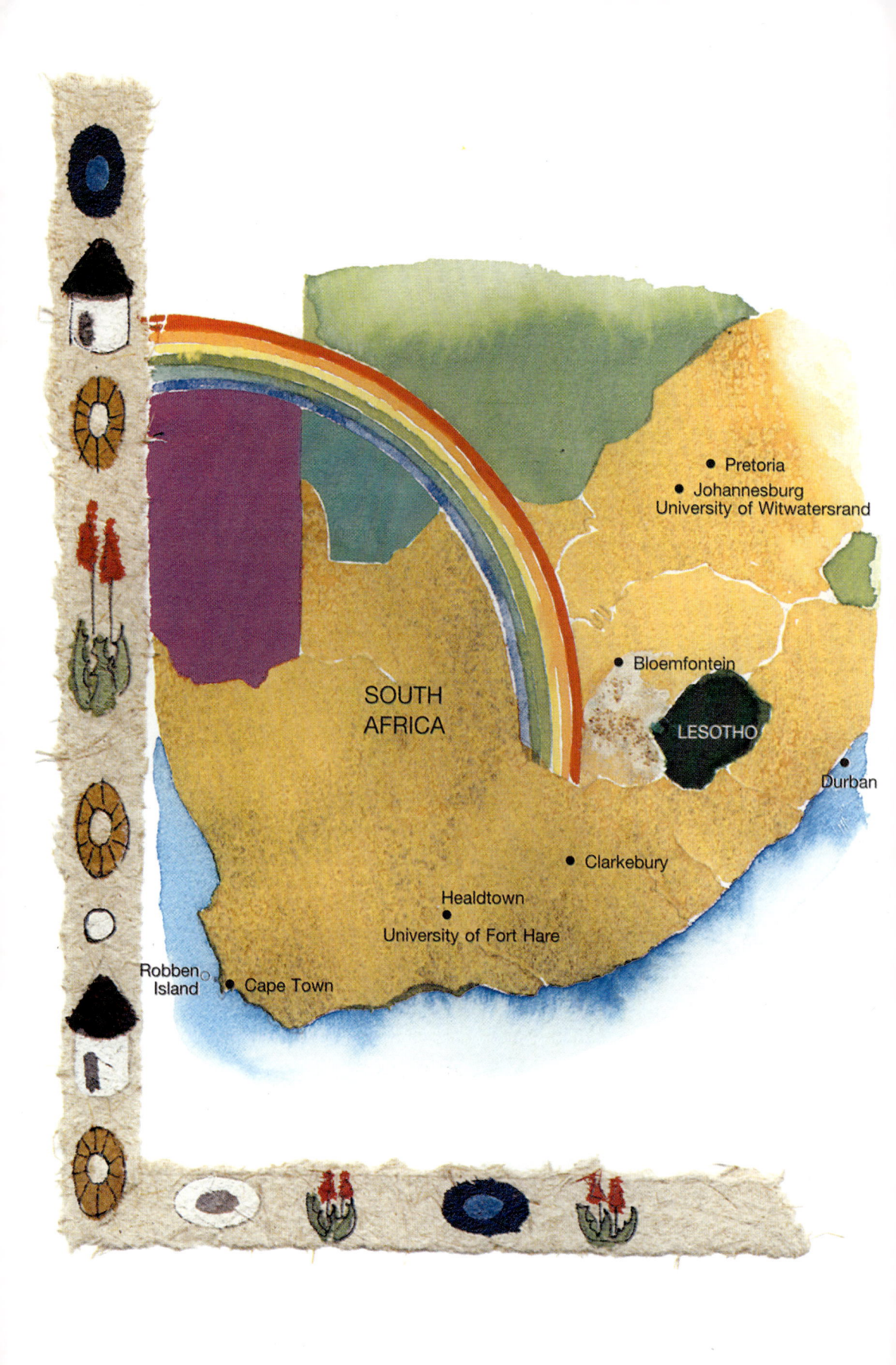

Pretoria
Johannesburg
University of Witwatersrand

Bloemfontein

LESOTHO

Durban

SOUTH AFRICA

Clarkebury

Healdtown
University of Fort Hare

Robben Island
Cape Town

Foreword

This is the story of Nelson Mandela as told by a Xhosa mine-worker to his children and their friends.

The story is told in this way because Nelson Mandela himself grew up hearing about the history of the Xhosa people from his own mother and father, who had heard it in turn from their parents. The legends, fables and stories of historic battles had a great effect on the boy.

In his book, Long walk to freedom, Nelson Mandela praises the efforts made by many men, women and children who worked – and died – in the struggle for freedom. In this way he has added to the wealth of stories being passed on from adult to child in the Xhosa tradition of story-telling. And just as he has passed on the stories of other people who took part in the struggle for freedom, so will others pass on the story of the greatest hero of all in South Africa's long walk to freedom.

Our story-teller is at home in the countryside for a few days before returning to the mines near Johannesburg, where he spends most of the year. The story of his personal walk to freedom may never be told – the freedom to live at home with his family and tell stories to his children every night of the year. For the time being it is enough that his young children and the children of his neighbours gather around the fire on a cold winter's night . . .

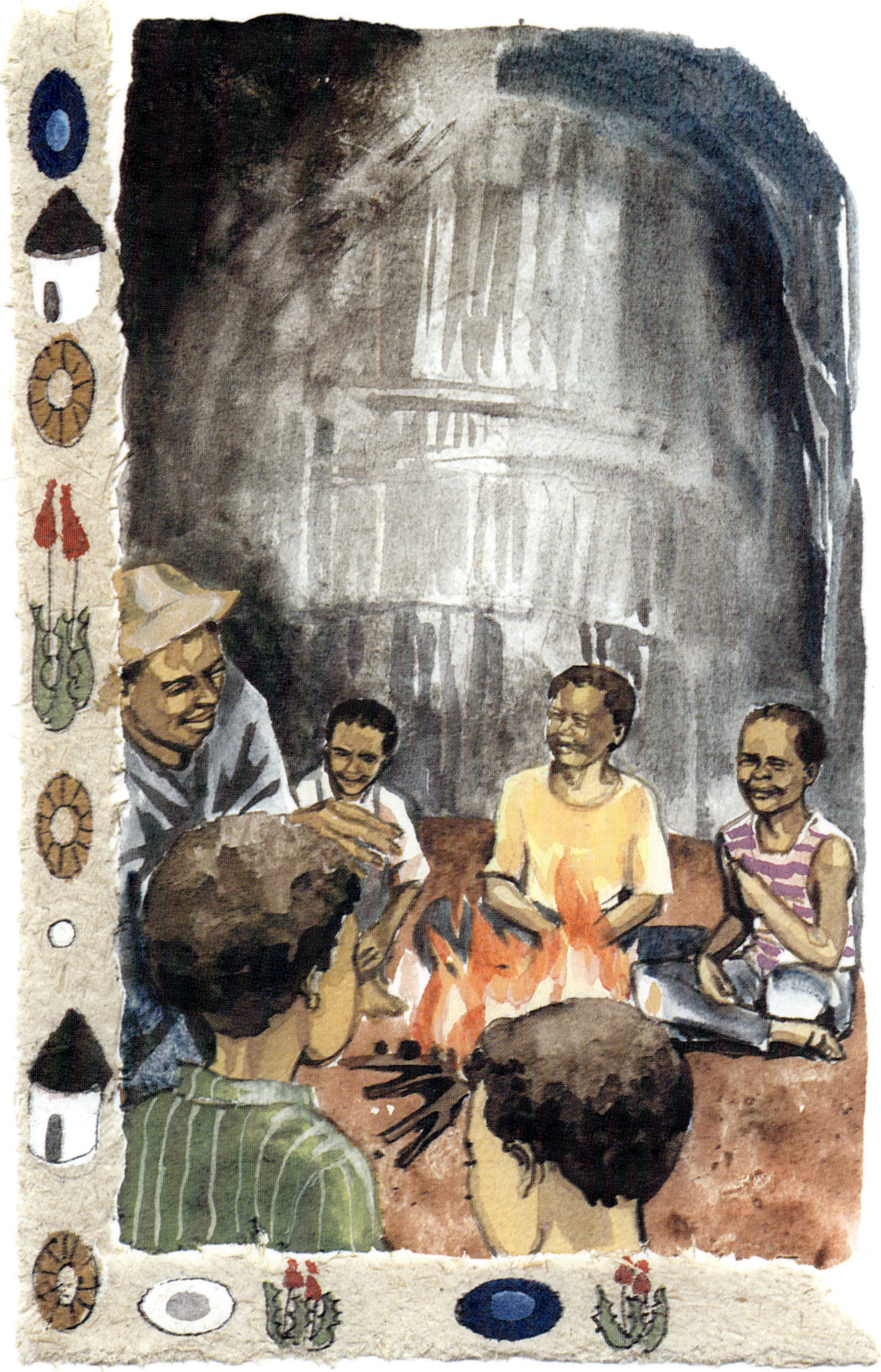

'Come and sit down my children, because tonight I want to tell you a story – a story of a great man.'

'Is it about a Xhosa warrior, Father? Or is it about a king or a giant? Tell us please!'

'I will, don't be so impatient; sit still and listen. It is about a great man who was born many years ago not far from here. And yes – in a way he is both a king and a giant. He is called Madiba.'

'Ah, our President, the President of South Africa, Nelson Mandela. Why is he called Madiba, Father?'

'All of us belong to a certain clan, as you know. Nelson's clan was called Madiba. To be called by the name of your clan is not only a term of respect but the highest honour a Xhosa can receive.'

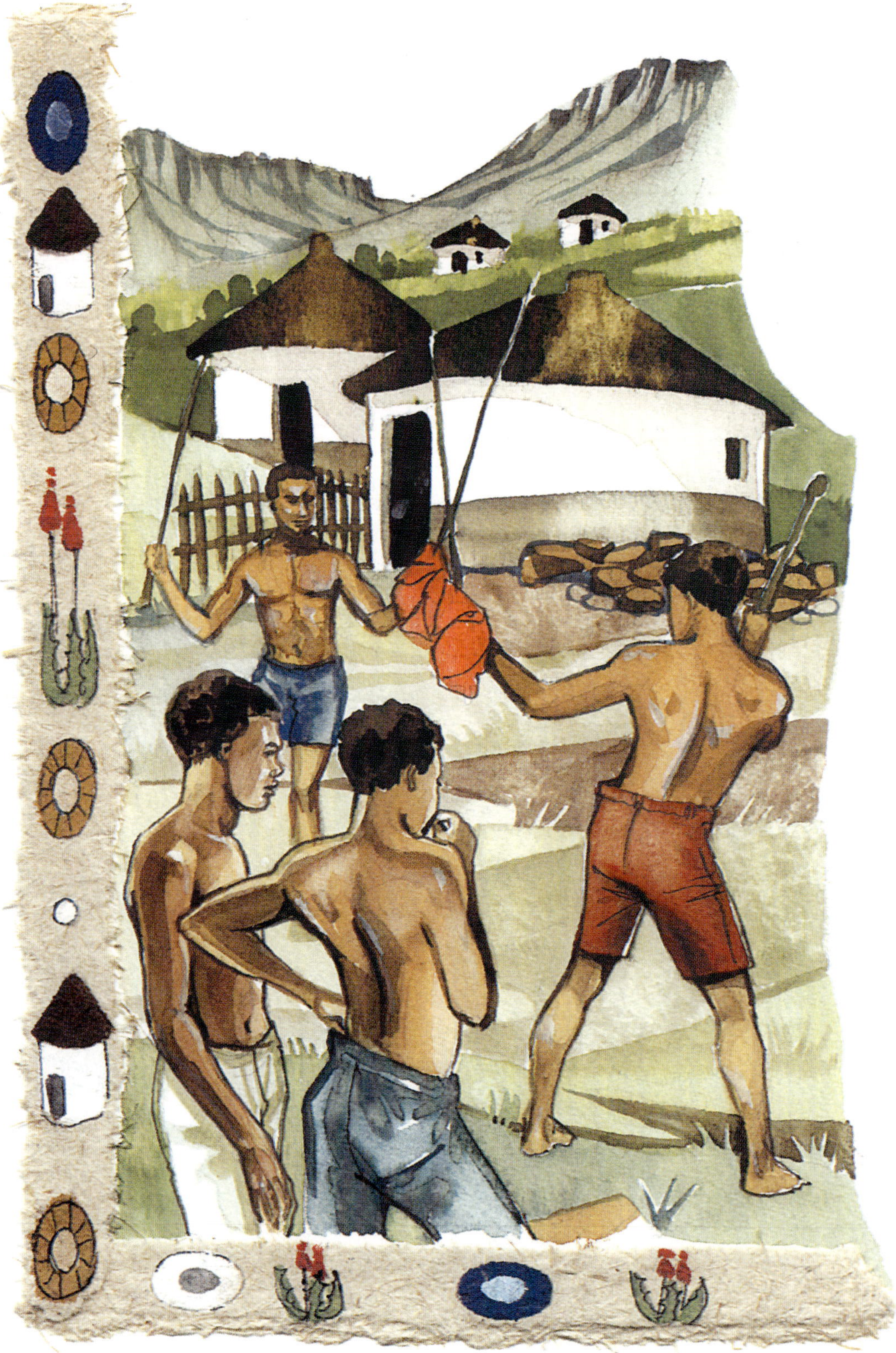

'Why do many people also call him Nelson, Father?'

'It is an English name, a Western name given to him by his first teacher. Perhaps she thought of the great British sea captain Lord Nelson, but Madiba isn't sure about this.'

'My father says Madiba has a thousand beautiful shirts given to him by many of his friends and my mother says she is very glad she doesn't have to wash and iron them!'

'It sounds like foolish talk to me, children. Always be careful about gossip. People often say untrue, hurtful things when they have nothing better to do. What does it matter if a man has one or a thousand shirts or no shirt at all? One can wear only one shirt at a time. It is what's inside the shirt that matters. When Madiba was a boy he wore a blanket just like some of you still sometimes do. And he also enjoyed playing and fighting with the other boys in the village. He learned to stick-fight, which helped him to become a good boxer later on in life.'

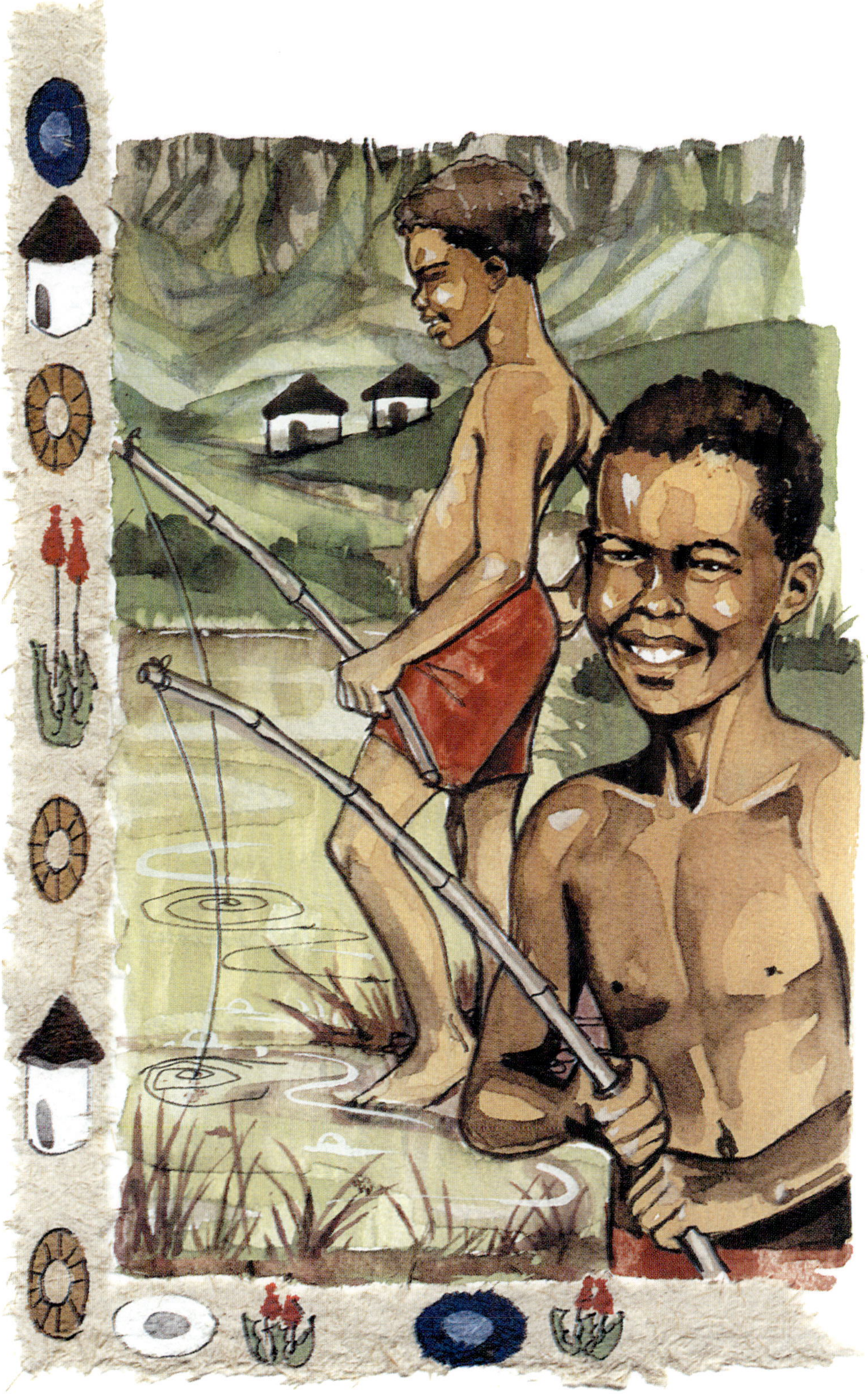

'Did he look after the sheep and the calves in the field?'

'Of course he did. He also gathered wild honey and fruits and used a sling-shot to knock birds out of the sky. He dug up edible vegetable roots and caught fish . . .'

'How do you know all of these things, Father?'

'A friend of mine in Johannesburg lent me a big book which Madiba wrote and I want you all to read it when you are older. It is called *Long Walk to Freedom*. There he tells us that his childhood was very much like yours — except that he wasn't allowed to ask so many questions.'

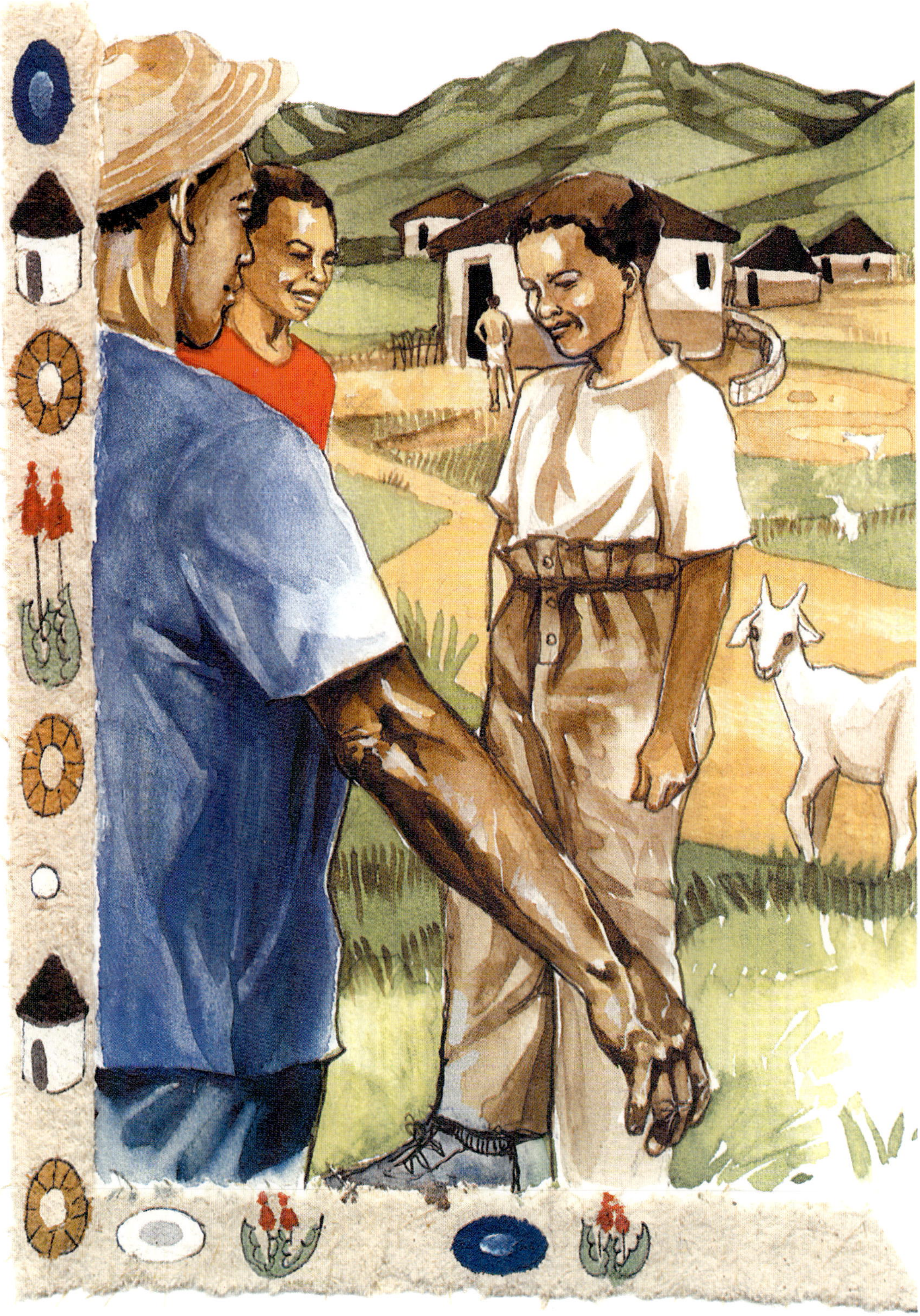

'Our teacher says it is good to ask questions, otherwise we won't learn the truth.'

'Perhaps so, but when Madiba was a boy it was different. Children were brought up more strictly and life was harder. Madiba had to make his own toys, like clay oxen. Do you know that his first pair of long pants came from his father? They were too big and too long but his father shortened them and tied them around Madiba's waist with a piece of string.'

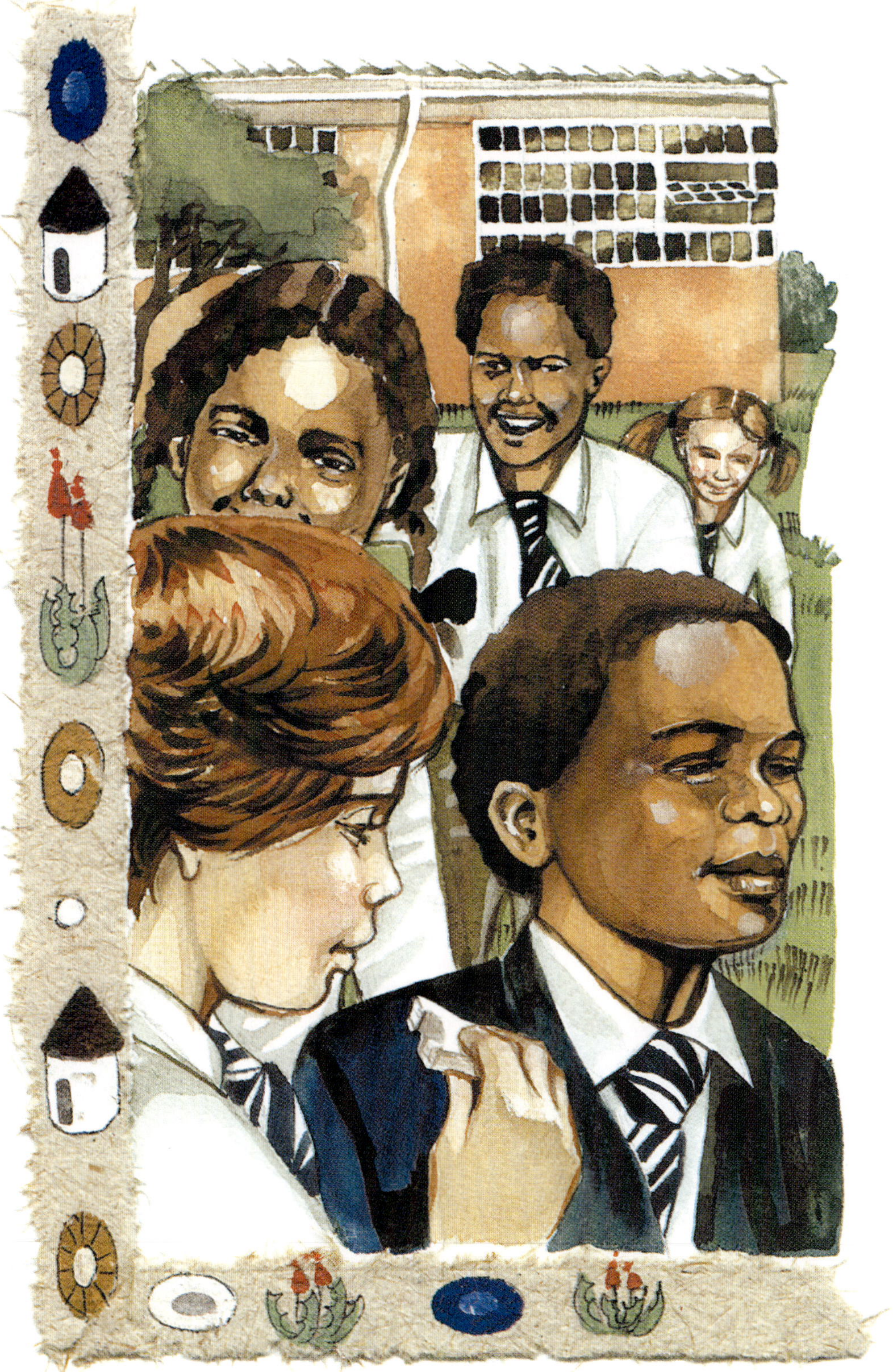

'Madiba must have looked very funny.'

'Of course he did, but you see, like the shirt we talked of earlier, it doesn't really matter what you wear as long as you have a good heart. I see many children in Johannesburg with bags full of books and they are dressed in expensive school uniforms. But I often hear that many of them do not work hard at school and get up to mischief, in spite of their privileges. Madiba says in his book that he has known many talented young people who have got nowhere because they had no discipline and no respect for traditions.'

'Perhaps it's also because they are not circumcised. Was Madiba circumcised, Father?'

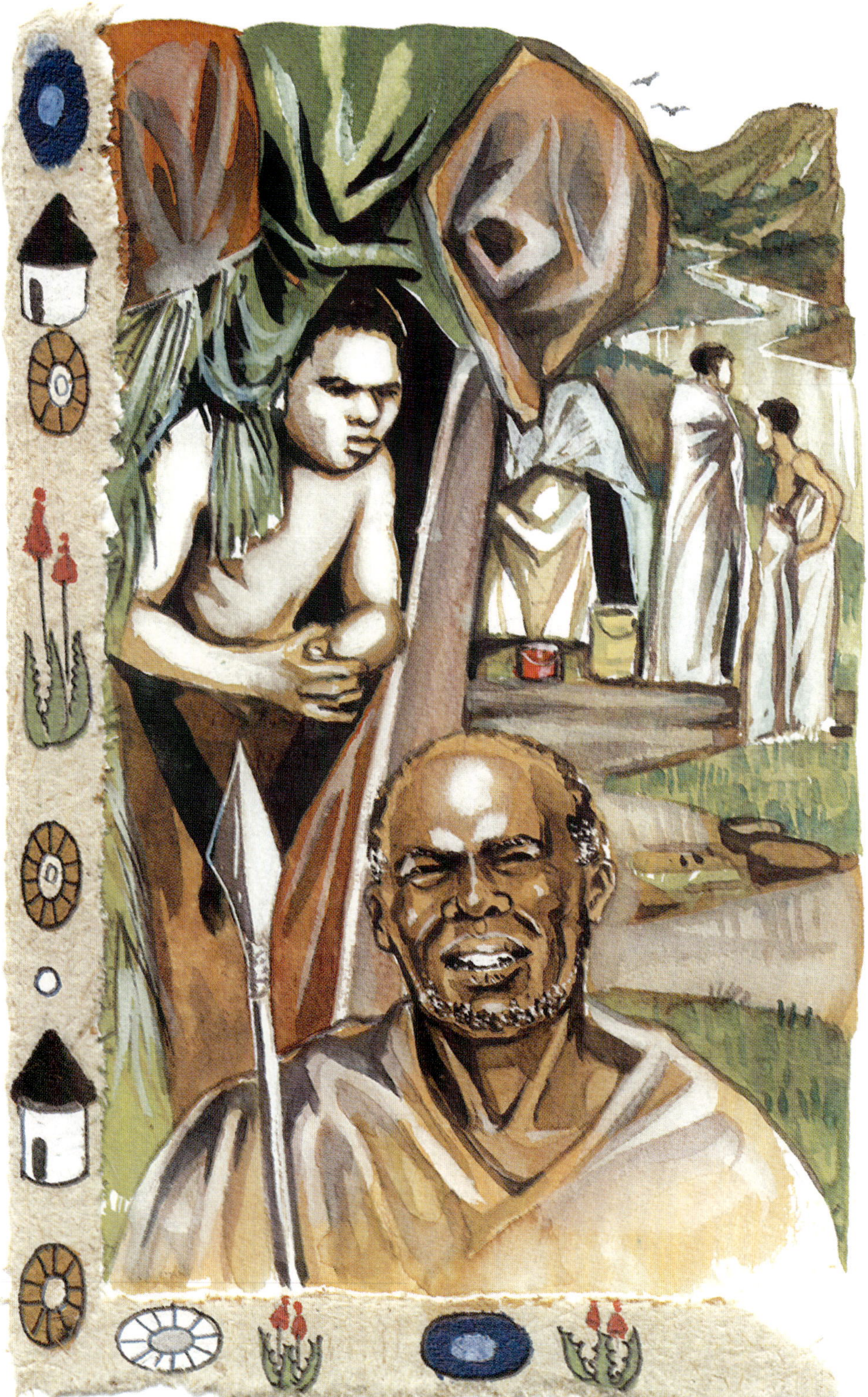

'Yes he was. You boys will also be circumcised in a few year's time. You know that it is our tradition . . . a Xhosa who is not circumcised is not a man. When Madiba and some other boys were sixteen, they spent some time in secluded huts to prepare for the ceremony. That is our custom. Early one morning an elderly man of the tribe used an assegai to change them from boys to men. That's what happened in those days, but today it's done differently.'

'Ouch – it must be very sore.'

'Yes, my son – it is. I know. But it makes you a man and a proud Xhosa. Madiba says he counts his years as a man from the date of his circumcision.'

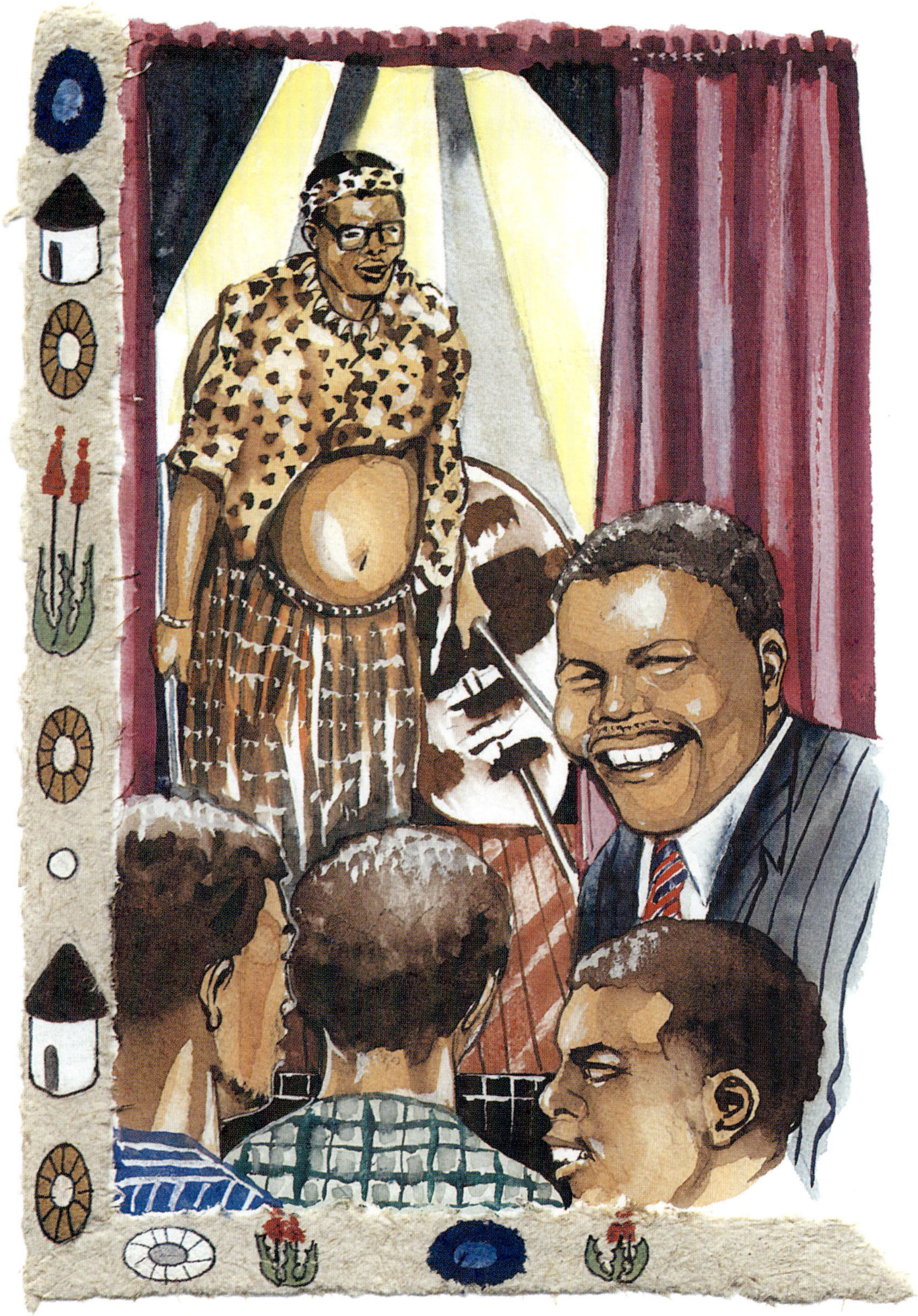

'So you can't be a president if you aren't circumcised?'

'Of course you can be. There are many people who aren't circumcised because it's not their tradition. Madiba went to school at Clarkebury and as a schoolboy he felt that there were many other pupils who were brighter, cleverer and stronger than he was. He decided that he would work very hard in order to succeed. When Madiba was nineteen he joined his friend, Justice, at a college called Healdtown. Justice was four years older than Madiba but they became the best of friends. During his final year at college, the Xhosa poet, Krune Mqhayi, spoke to the students. He was dressed in a leopard skin kaross and a matching hat.'

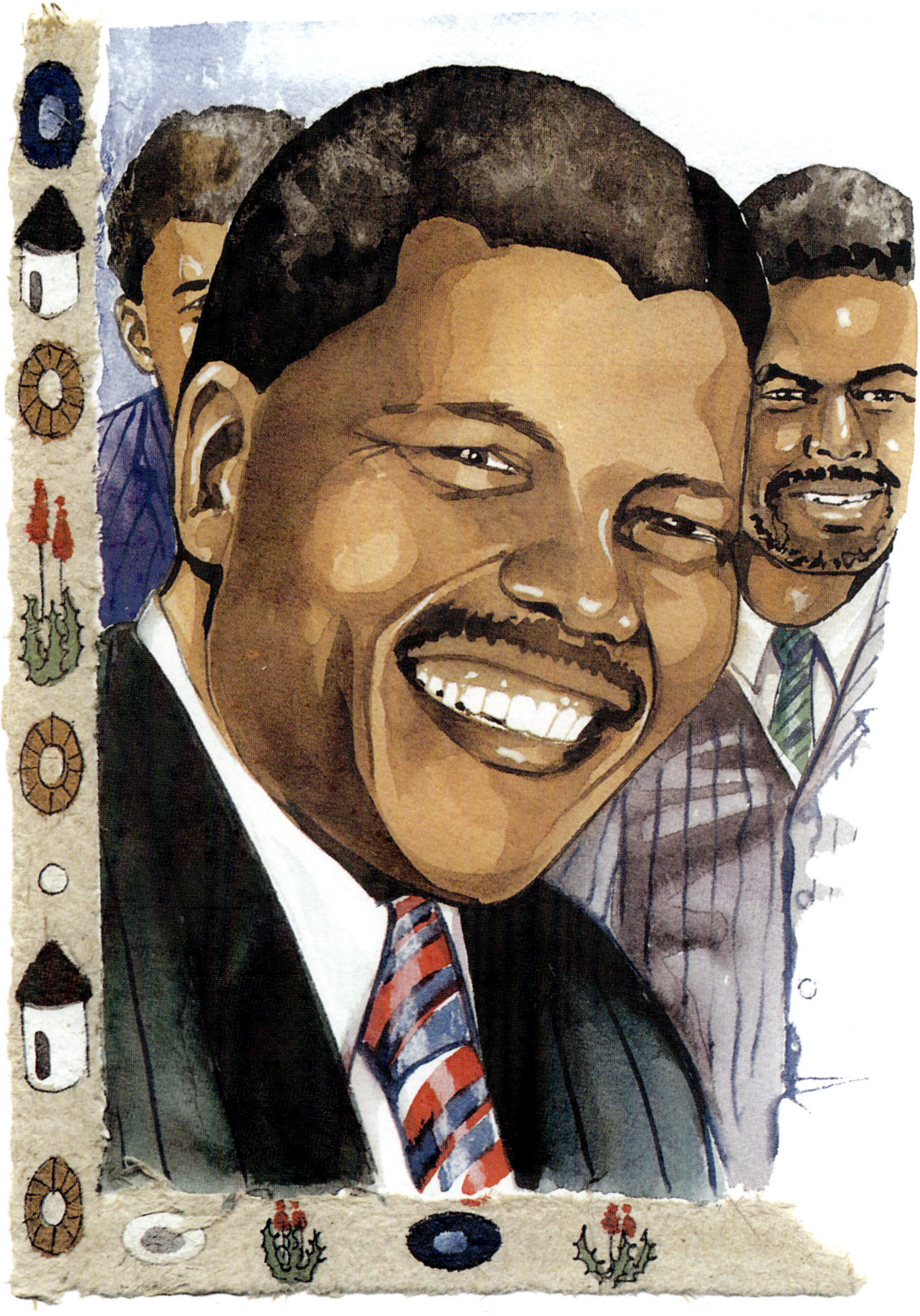

'It must be warm to wear a leopard skin in winter instead of a blanket, Father. I'd love to wear one.'

'I'd like a leopard skin too, but we can't just kill all of them for their skins. There were many leopards when Madiba was a boy but there are not so many left today. Anyway, the students were not there to look at the poet's kaross. They wanted to hear what he had to say. It was almost as if Krune Mqhayi saw into the future when he told them that the people of Africa would one day achieve a victory over the oppressor who did not care for what is African and good. This speech made a great impression on the young Madiba.'

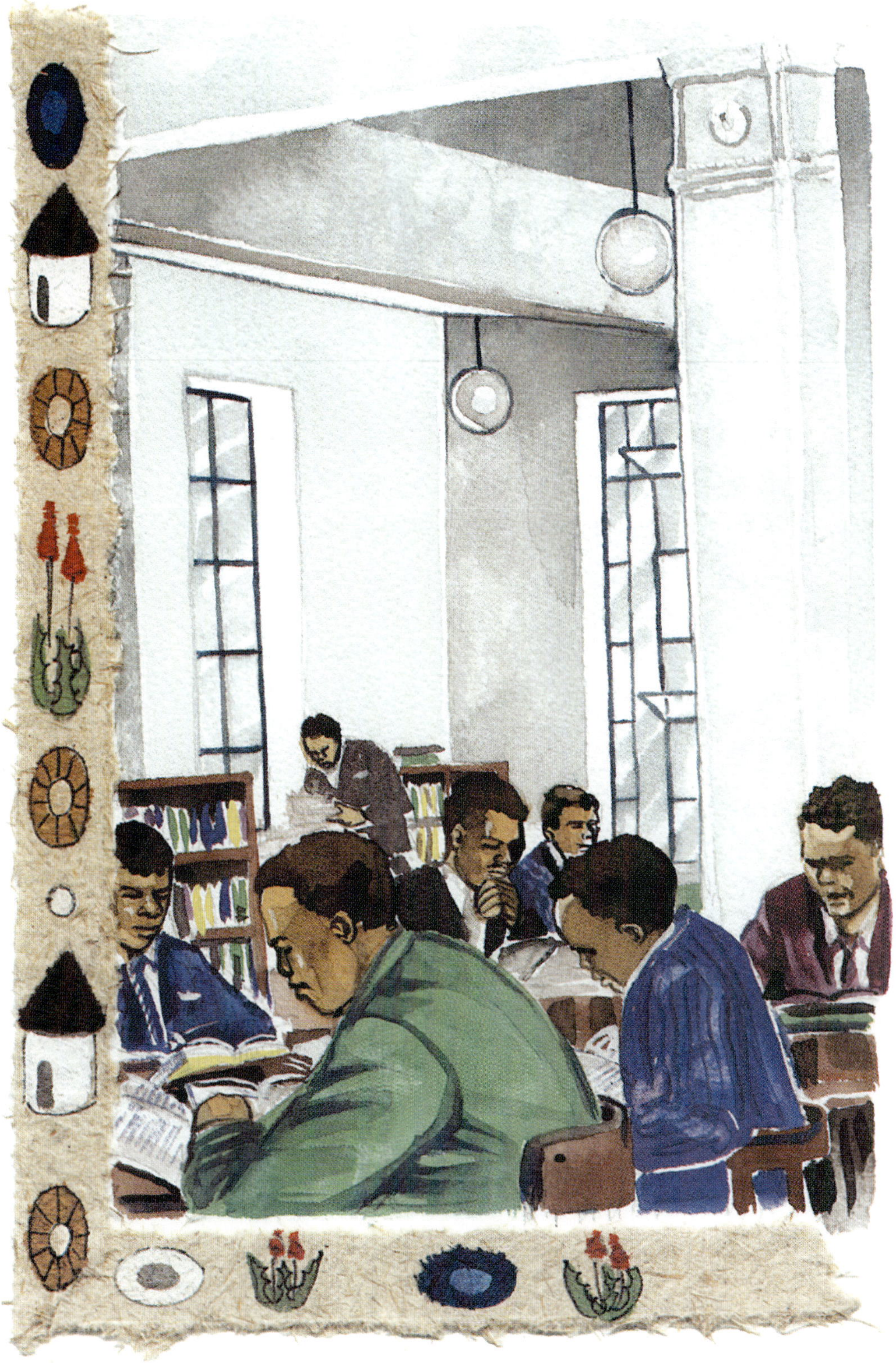

'He and Justice went to Fort Hare University. They passed the first year exams. But then the regent, the ruler of the Xhosas, told them that he had arranged for them to be married to two girls chosen from good families. Madiba and Justice did not want this. They had too many dreams and unfinished business. They didn't want to be tied down yet. So they decided to run away to Johannesburg.'

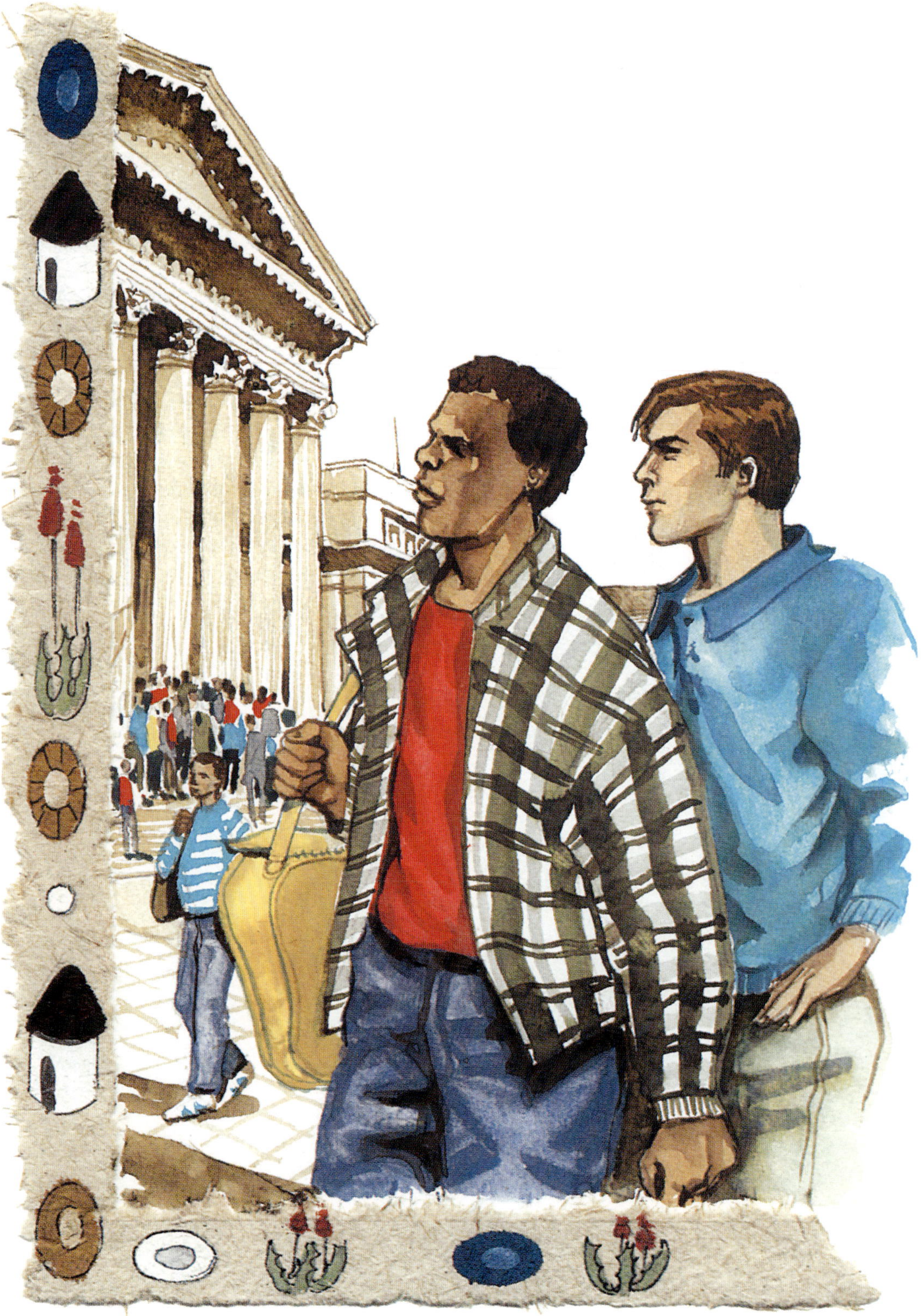

'Is that why he called his book Long Walk to Freedom, Father?'

'No, not really. The long, hard walk to freedom took Madiba nearly his whole life. I will tell you later about the real freedom he looked for. In Johannesburg Madiba and Justice had no jobs and very little money, but fortunately Justice knew some people who were very kind to them: black, white, coloured and Indian people who sympathised with people who were oppressed and exploited. They helped Madiba to go to Wits University and finish his studies so that he could become a lawyer.'

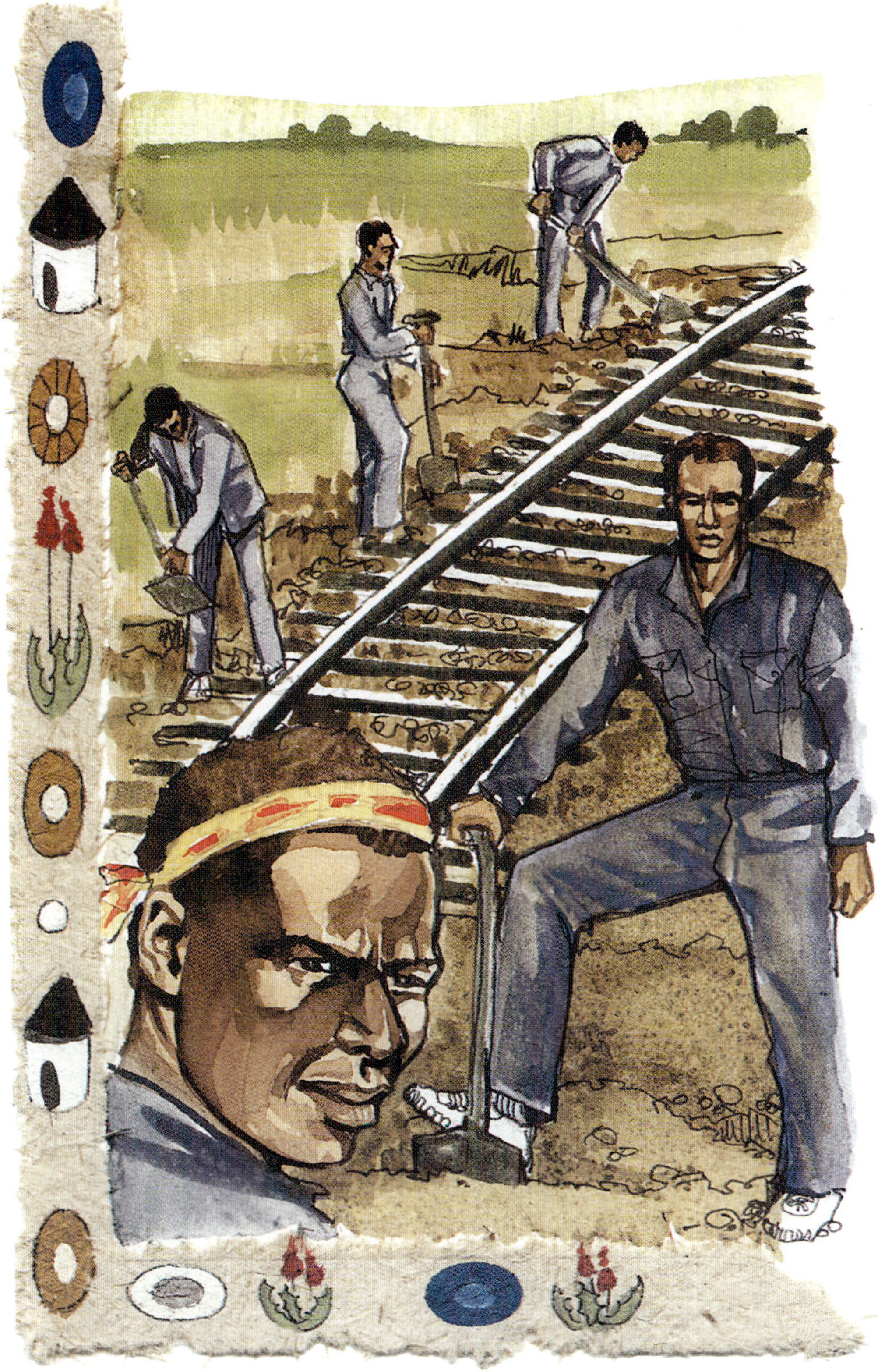

'You sometimes use words we don't understand, Father. What do you mean by oppressed and exploited?'

'These are words that mean many things, but when you are oppressed you are kept down by force. You are not free to work and live where you please. Other people decide what is good for you, whether it is fair or unfair. And when you are exploited, your oppressors make you work very long hours. They get rich while you remain poor.'

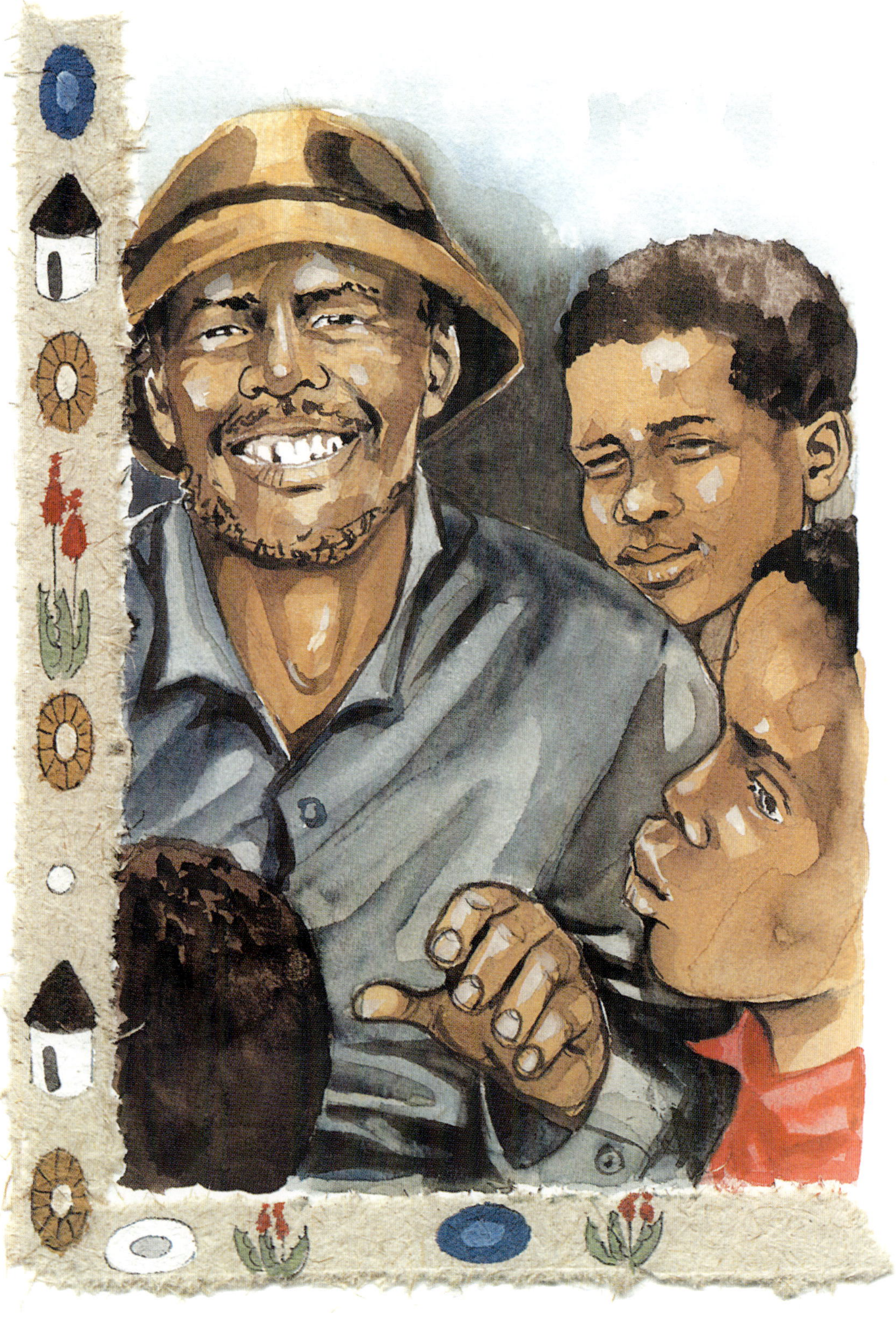

'My grandfather says he worked very hard all his life, but now he is still a poor man.'

'He is not the only one, my son. I can tell you all night about the struggle and how hard it was for Madiba and all his helpers to see that everybody should be treated fairly. But it will be better if you read about that in Madiba's book. You will then understand what it means to have freedom.'

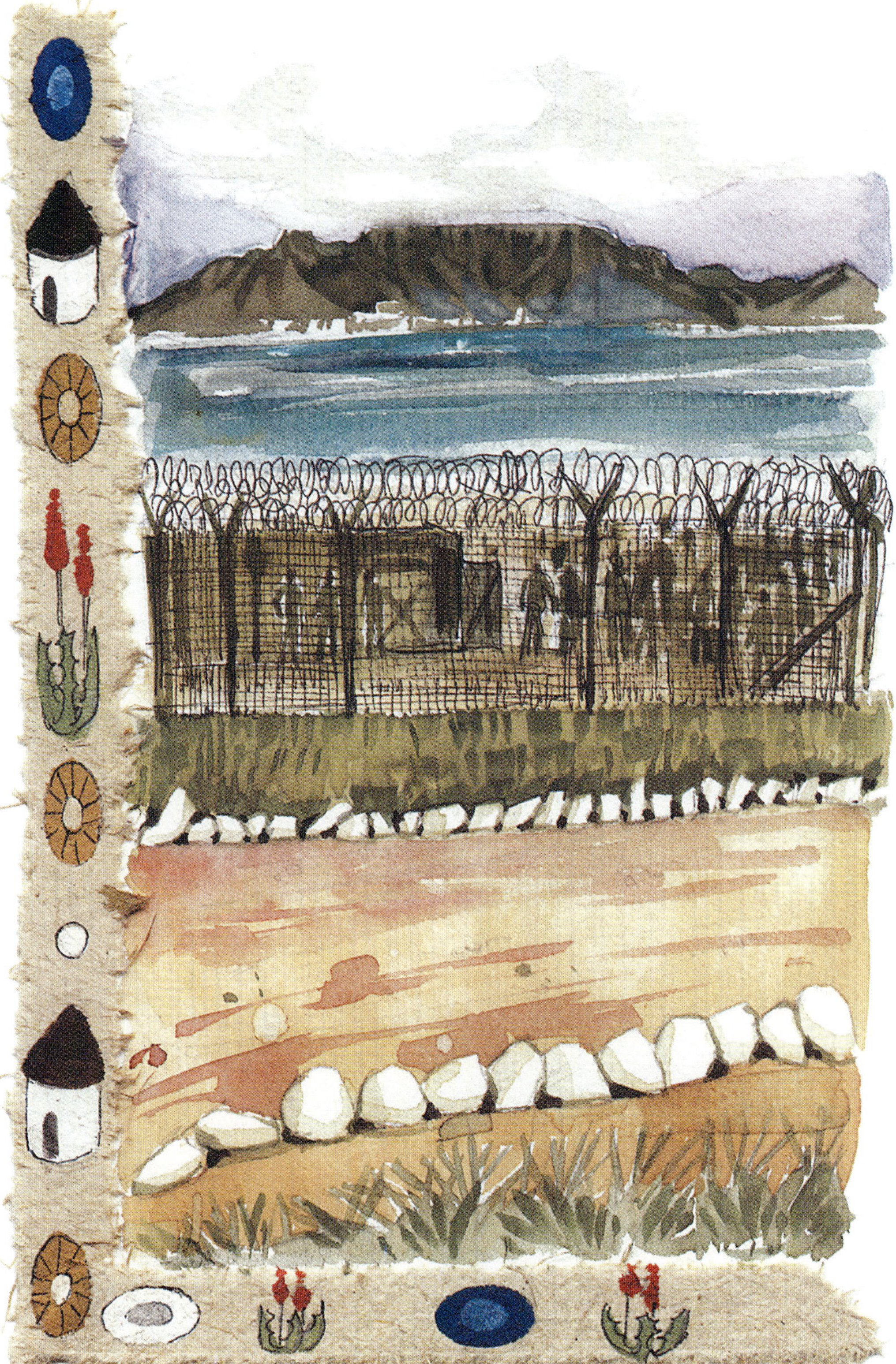

'And was Madiba put into prison because he wanted black people to be free, Father?'

'Yes, my son. He spent 27 years of his life in several prisons because he wanted everybody to be free, not only black people! He believed strongly that unless everybody is free – nobody is free. He spent many of those years chopping limestone on an island that was icy-cold and windswept in winter and as hot as this fire in summer. This place is called Robben Island.'

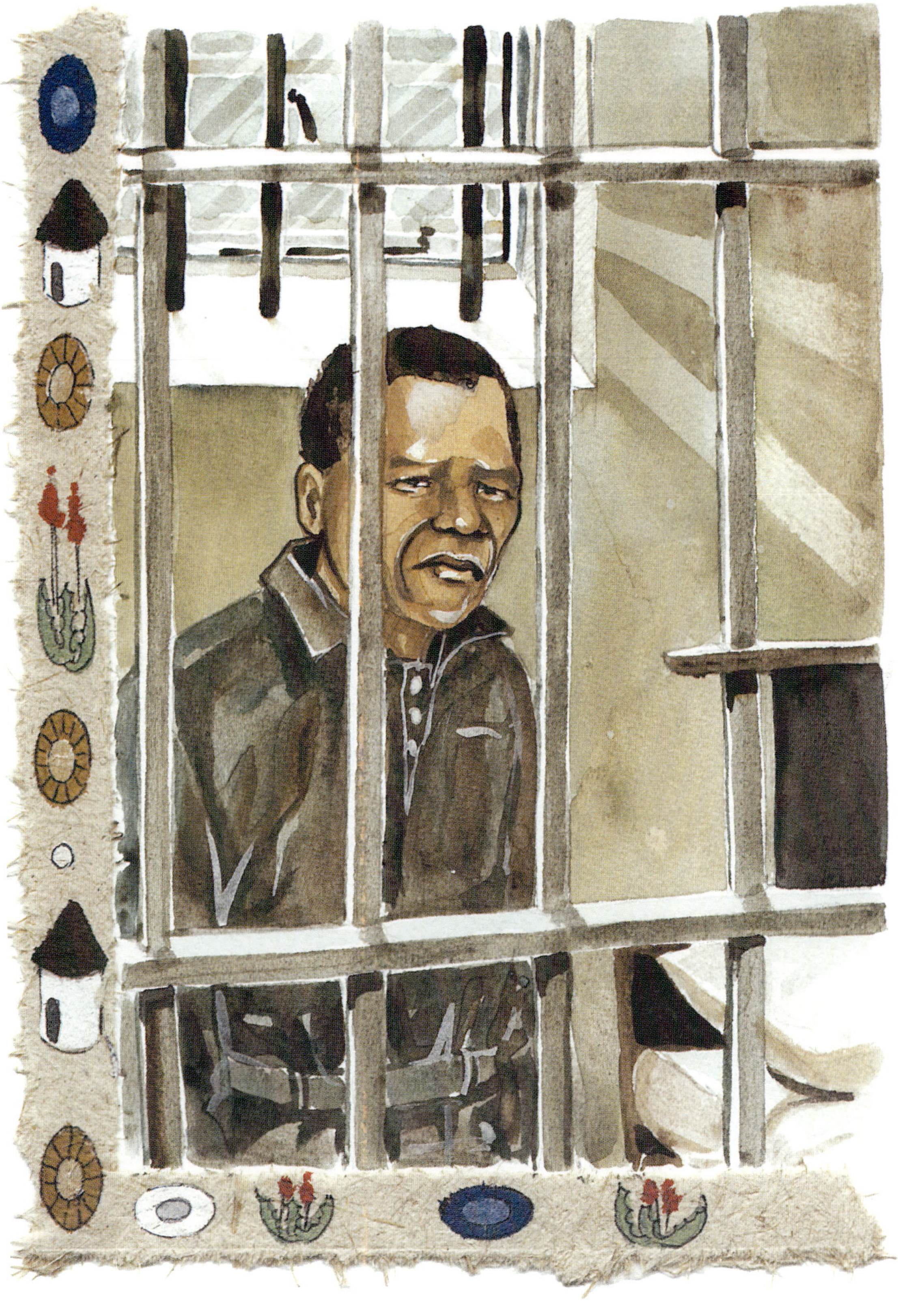

'But, my children, if you put an honest man in prison, even for fifty years, you will not kill his dream — a dream to see that all people have the same rights and opportunities . . . that all people are free.'

'I would be very angry if they put me in prison just because I wanted all people to be free, Father.'

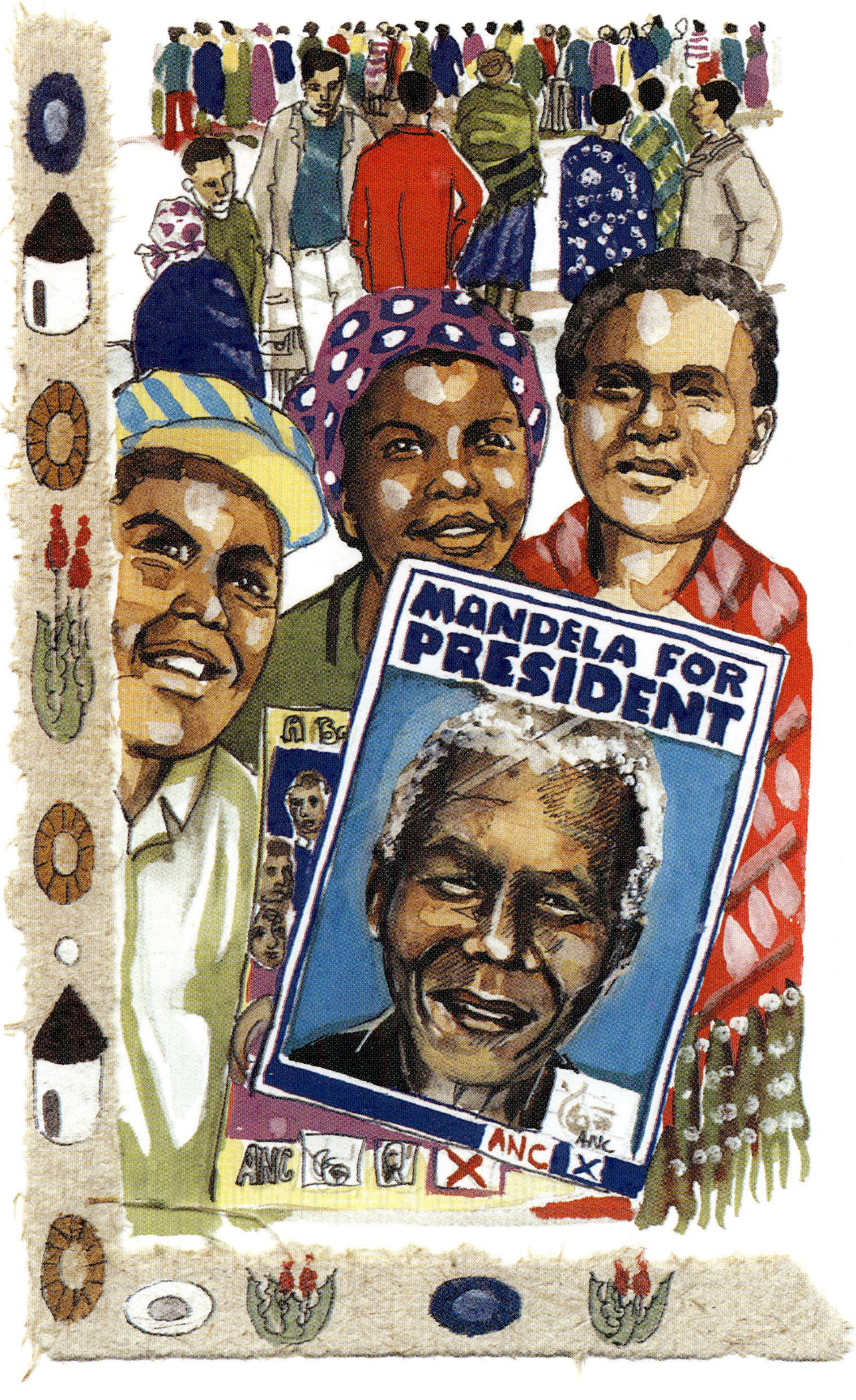
MANDELA FOR
PRESIDENT
ANC
ANC

'I agree. So would I. But Madiba is not an ordinary person. If you are angry, even if you have good reason, you often do or say things that will not solve problems – you make them worse. When Madiba came out of prison, he realised that the only way to make South Africa a better land was to try to forgive those linked to bad things of the past and to get everybody, old and young, to work together for the good of all.'

'That was in 1990! We listened on the radio. We were very, very happy. Where were you that day, Father?'

'I was with my friends in the mine hostel. We watched Madiba's release on television. Afterwards we ran out into the township streets. Everyone in Soweto was outside, dancing and singing songs. I will never forget what it led to in 1994. Can you tell me what that was, children?'

'The people voted, Father!'

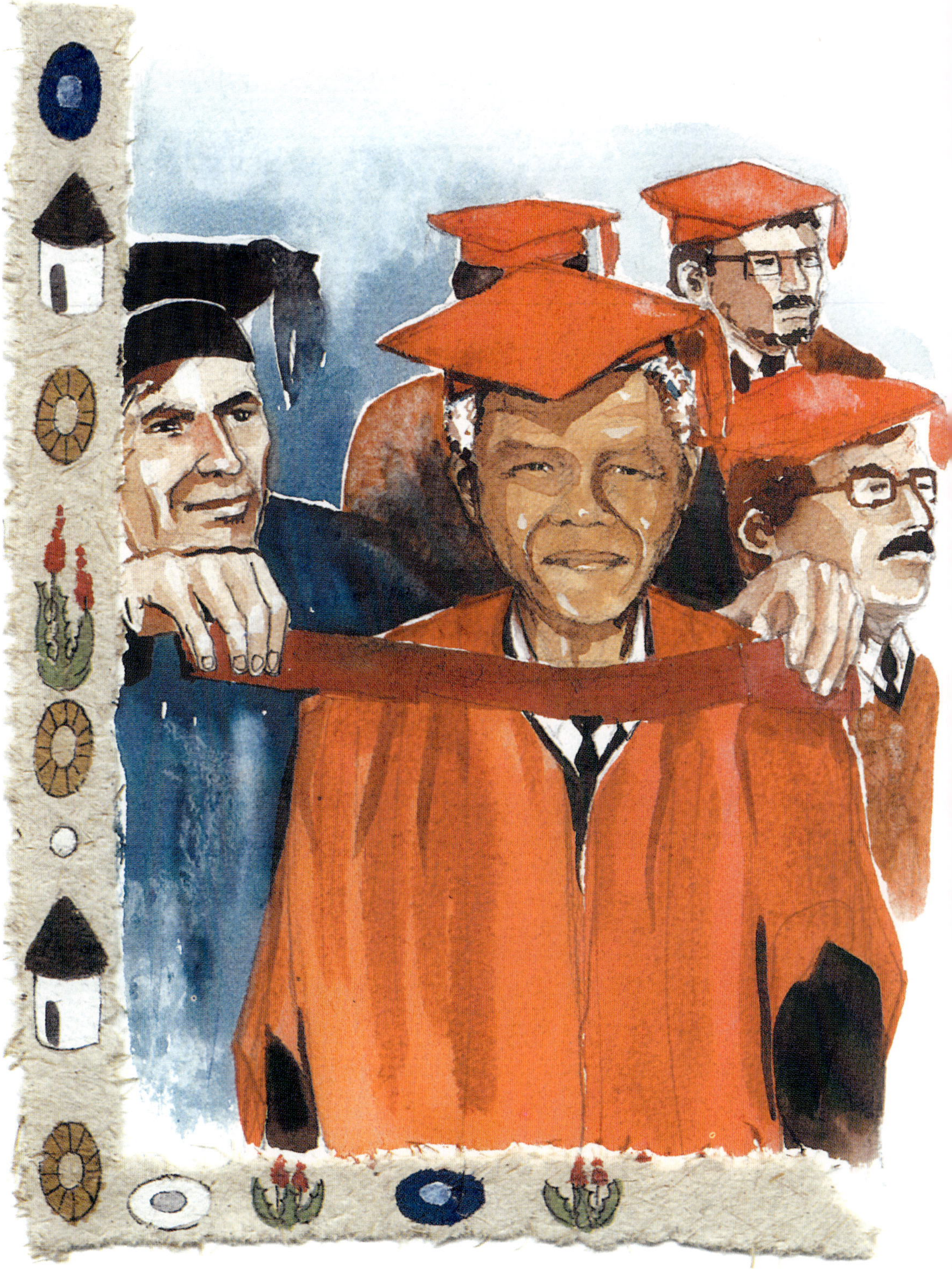

'Yes, my son. For the first time in South African history, *everybody* was allowed to vote and it was no surprise that most people voted for Madiba. And all over the world, wherever Madiba goes now, he is praised and respected for being . . . perhaps the greatest leader of our time. Many universities have made him a Doctor of this and a Doctor of that . . . twenty or thirty times, I do not know . . .'

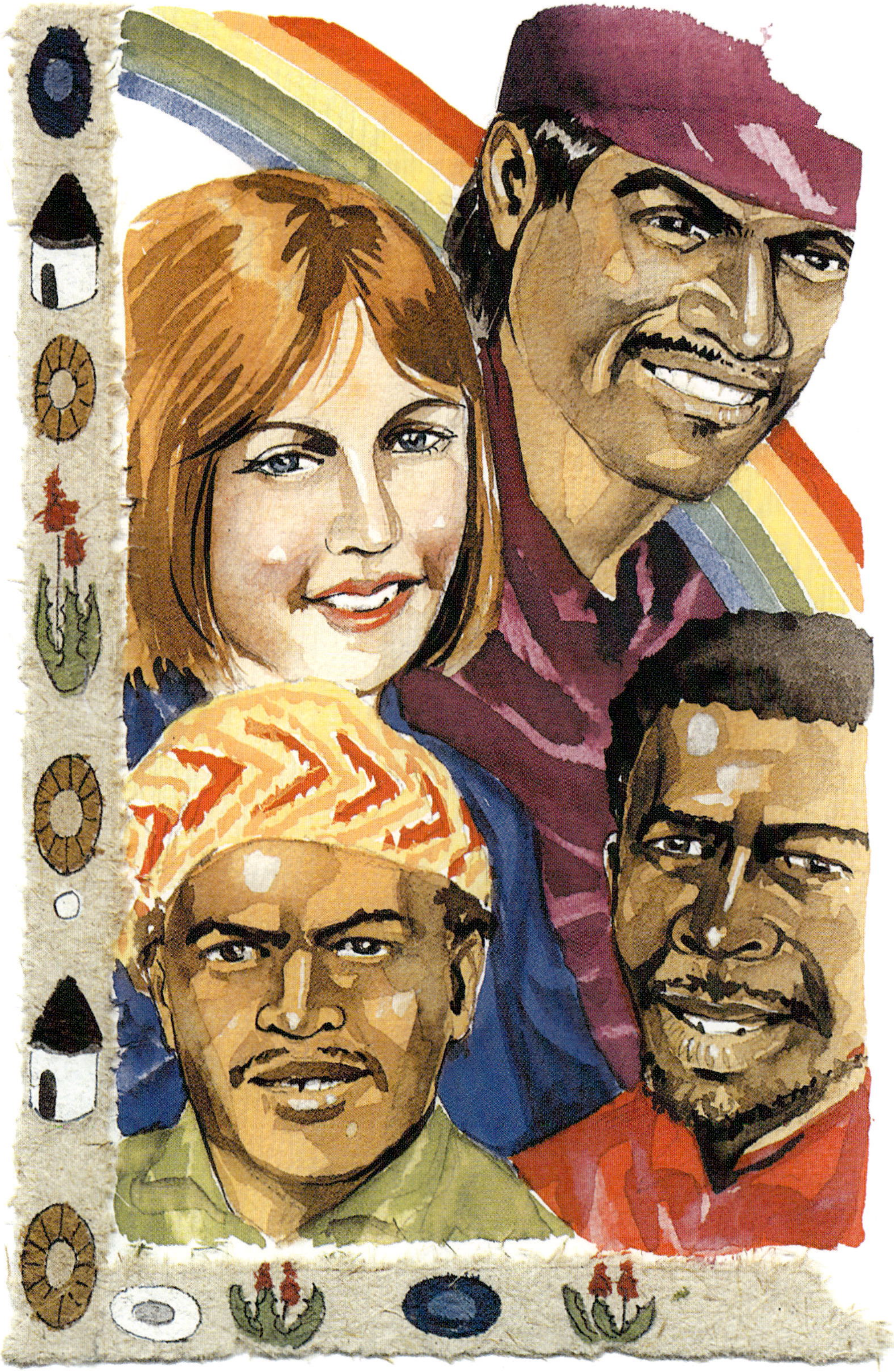

'I wish Madiba would cure my grandfather. He worked in the mines when he was young and now he is very sick and coughs in the night.'

'Well, my boy. Madiba is not a Doctor of medicine. He is a Doctor of Law, of Justice, who tries to cure the ills of our nation – of all the people of South Africa.'

'The rainbow nation, Father?'

'Yes, exactly . . . the rainbow nation . . . but it's not easy. You see, there are many good people and many bad people . . . selfish, cruel, lazy, greedy, dishonest people . . . and Madiba is trying to heal them . . . he is that sort of Doctor.'

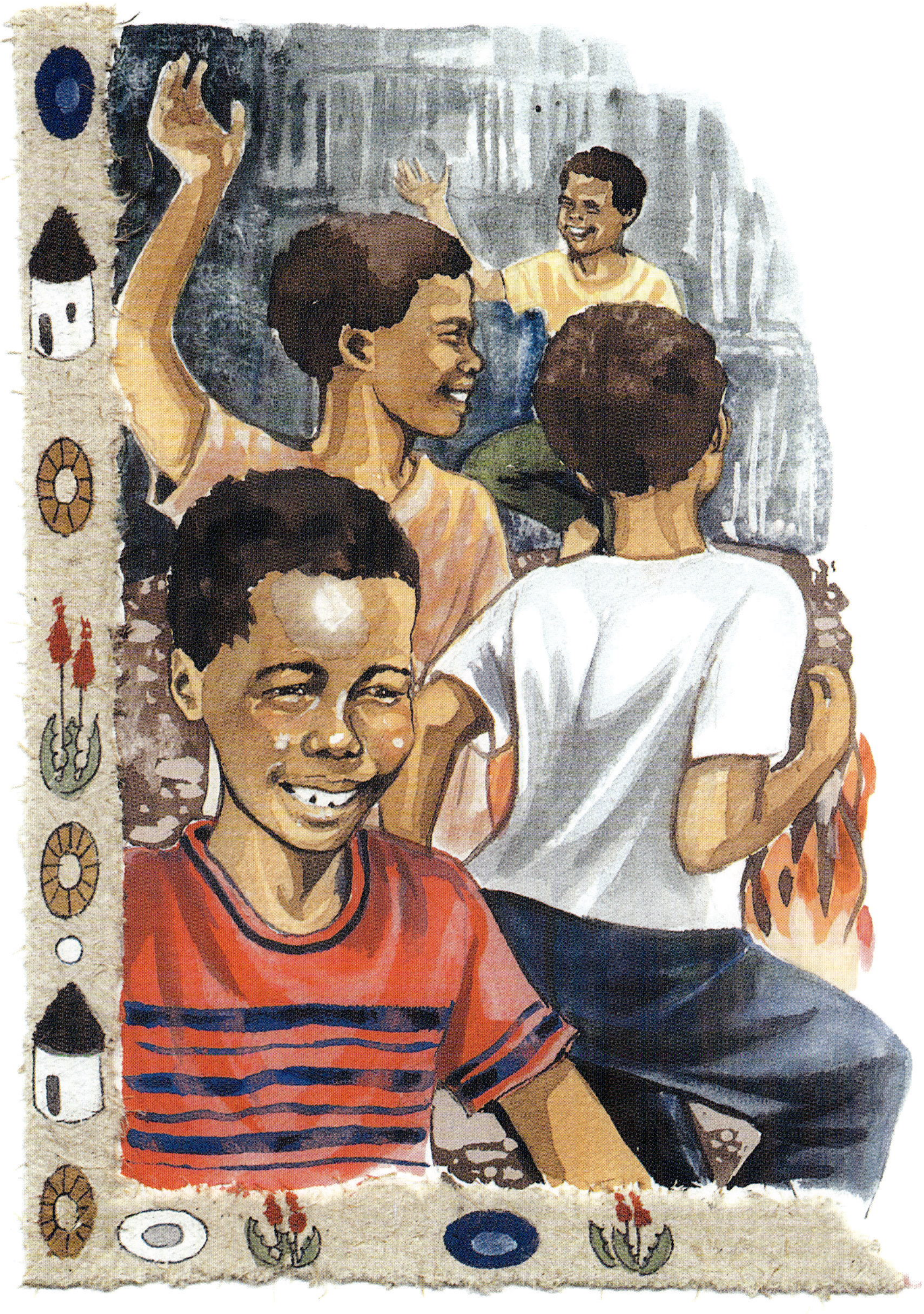

'But can I also be a doctor when I grow up, Father?'

'It won't be so difficult for you, my son. You won't have to spend 27 years in prison to become a Doctor of Justice, or Medicine or whatever, because Madiba has changed all that. It's really quite simple. You must just stand up for the rights of *all people* . . . obey the law, be honest, work hard and have concern for others . . . especially old people and those less fortunate than you are. You should never become bitter, even if people treat you badly – very badly. Help wherever you can, even if it's only a friendly smile – it costs nothing. Always try to keep peace in your heart. That's more important than anything else. Like Madiba – you must be a man of peace! It is getting late – let us sing and go to bed.'

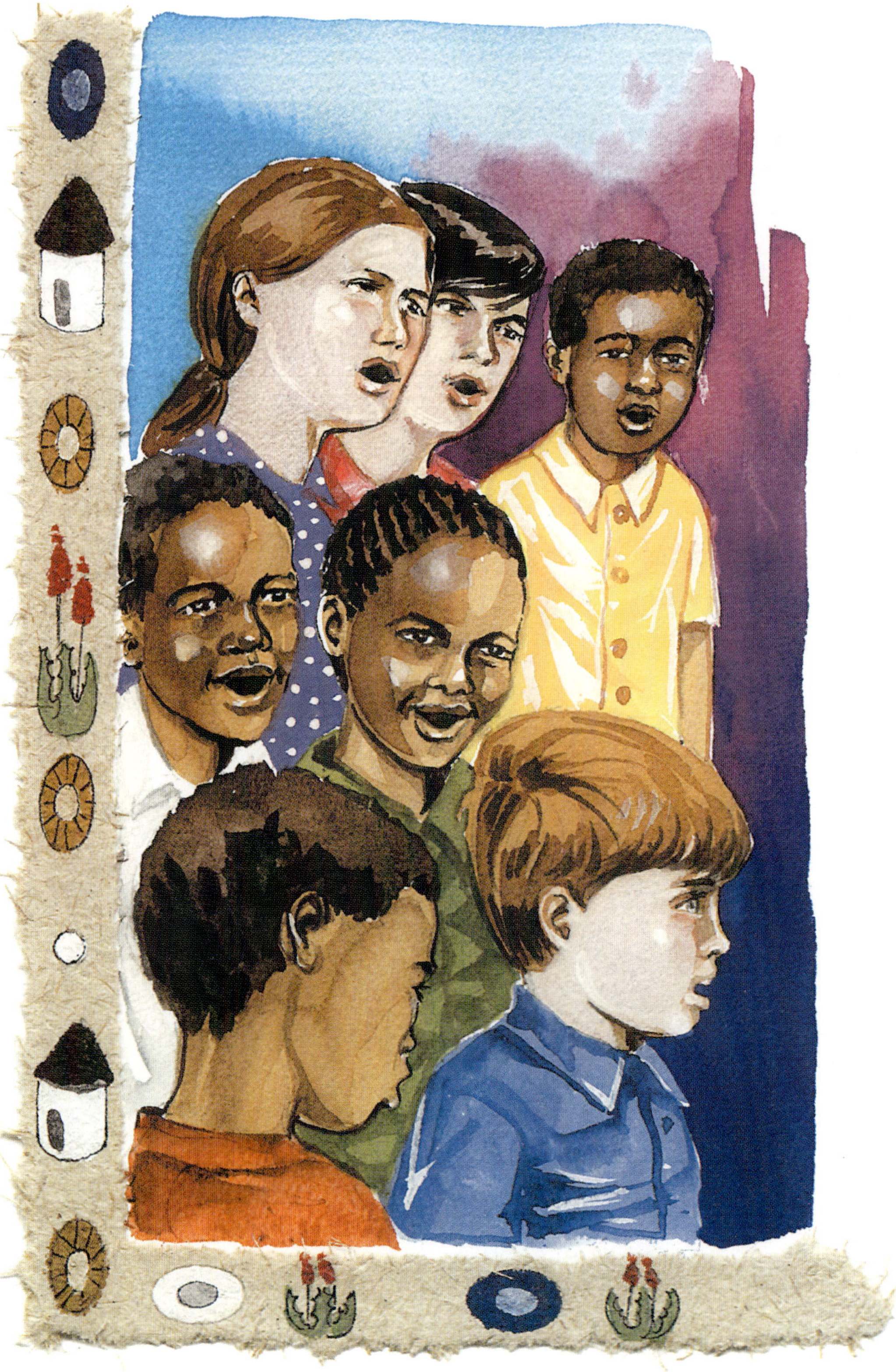

Nkosi sikelel' i-Afrika
Maluphakanyisw' uphondo lwayo
Yizwa imithandazo yethu
Nkosi sikelela thina lusapho lwayo

Morena boloka Setjhaba sa heso
O fedise dintwa lematshwenyeho
O se boloke
O se boloke
Setjhaba sa heso
Setjhaba sa South Africa
South Africa

Uit die blou van onse hemel
Uit die diepte van ons see
Oor ons ewige gebergtes
Waar die kranse antwoord gee

Sounds the call to come together
And united we shall stand
Let us live and strive for freedom
In South Africa our land.

| d : d | m : m | s : — | s : s . l | t : l . s | l : r |

e- wi- ge ge- berg- tes waar die kran- se ant- woord

| s : — | : m . s | l : l | m : m | s : — | s : s . f |

gee, Sounds the call to come to- ge- ther, and u-

| m : m | l : f | r : — | : d ., m | s : s | s : d' |

ni- ted we shall stand, Let us live and strive for

| d' : — | l : s .. f | m : s | l : t | d' : — : — |

free- dom in South- A- fri- ca our Land.

E.Sontonga, arr.M.Khumalo (Nkosi)
Afrikaans words: C.J.Langenhoven
English words: J.Z-Rudolph

M.L.de Villiers, arr.D.de Villiers (Die Stem)

Re-arrangement, music typesetting-Jeanne Z.Rudolph
as per Anthem Committee